FAILURE AND I BURY THE BODY

THE NATIONAL POETRY SERIES

The *National Poetry Series* was established in 1978 to ensure the publication of five poetry books annually through five participating publishers. Publication is funded by the Lannan Foundation; Stephen Graham; Joyce & Seward Johnson Foundation; Juliet Lea Hillman Simonds; The Poetry Foundation; and Olafur Olafsson.

2012 COMPETITION WINNERS

the meatgirl whatever, by Kristin Hatch of San Francisco, CA
Chosen by K. Silem Mohammad, to be published by Fence Books

The Narrow Circle, by Nathan Hoks of Chicago, IL
Chosen by Dean Young, to be published by Penguin Books

The Cloud That Contained the Lightning, by Cynthia Lowen of Brooklyn, NY
Chosen by Nikky Finney, to be published by University of Georgia Press

Visiting Hours at the Color Line, by Ed Pavliæ of Athens, GA
Chosen by Dan Beachy-Quick, to be published by Milkweed Editions

Failure and I Bury the Body, by Sasha West of Austin, TX
Chosen by D. Nurkse, to be published by HarperCollins Publishers

FAILURE
AND I BURY THE BODY

POEMS

SASHA WEST

HARPER PERENNIAL

NEW YORK • LONDON • TORONTO • SYDNEY • NEW DELHI • AUCKLAND

HARPER PERENNIAL

HarperCollins books may be purchased for educational, business, or sales promotional use. For information please e-mail the Special Markets Department at SPsales@harpercollins.com.

FIRST EDITION

Designed by Michael Correy

Library of Congress Cataloging-in-Publication Data is available upon request.

ISBN 978-0-06-227343-7

13 14 15 16 17   OV/RRD   10 9 8 7 6 5 4 3 2 1

For Charlie

Failure's Accounting of Titles

FAILURE AND I BURY THE BODY

Failure and I Take a Road Trip

Because Failure asked and I said yes,

Because I thought the spring would be beautiful, but being winter, was hidden,

Because I felt the pull to movement, to a belief in motion,

Because Failure had dark kind eyes and asked quietly,
And because I said yes,

Yes to the desert and to decay,

Yes to the ring I tattooed around my finger in numbers,

And yes, yes, to keeping all my ghosts in cages, like rabid ferrets, tying them
behind the car so they jostled and sang like cans,

And yes to the just-married exes,

And yes to the lost jobs, because, and yes,

I carried my suitcase to the car, and his trunks, and we packed woolen
smallpoxed blankets, and we packed bottled water, and oil, and oil,
and petrol, and provisions, and we fastened the latches on the black doors

And drove.

What It Used to Be Like:

Every rabbit in the field brought me luck.
Every rabbit arrived at my door with a basket of Luck, extended in their little
    furry paws.
I invited them in and took their wooden baskets.
I sat them down.
Then, I skinned each one for a coat, studded with their lucky feet, studded
    with the paws
they used to bring me luck in.

Road, Day One

Stretched along the dirt road, men and women without shoes, glass cases on their backs bearing shrines.

Violently lunatic and beautiful.

Pilgrimage in which we move from cattle car to dirt hole, in which we quench our thirst with irradiated water.

Shriven, covered in lace or a plastic tarp, the delicately carved madonnas swing with the gait of the walking. She swings against the force of their prayers. Lace. Plastic curtains. Barbed-wire finials. Chain-link table.

Fragua con estrellas.

Forge with the Stars of Distant Fire

Failure needs someone else, can't manage on his own, blinks into and
out of existence.

We go from motel to motel, most with signs shot out, a frame where the
name might be, jagged.

I care for him first disinterestedly like a nurse, then like a sister, hand on his
forehead, then like a lover, curled over his thigh in the bed—

He shudders and revels in the delicious feeling of being wrong.

Downed telephone pole hit by a car
Sluggish god who wrestles

At night, we hold a handful of flares out the window, headlights off, to see
the rabbits run alongside us, to watch the sage pass.

Scrub weeds bring the self to the forefront of the conscious vision,
The world gets windier.

I brought a sack of earth with me from my home and every night I eat a
mouthful

While the men dig history out of the ground and scatter it—

Flint chips in lunch boxes and desk drawers across the suburban swathe

The past drawn out from the sere hills.

Yes, That Year.

While bees disappeared from loaded boxes on trucks,
bodies giving out from the brute force of flight, shuttled
from one orchard to the next, one field to another, while pollen
still across cities deposited its silt over sleepers and buildings, while the world
warmed slowly, I took in the stray dog of Failure.

Smog & rising floods, the large fish gone.

Hadn't I taken in that cat, all ribs, beset by how it would lay its starved body
    at my door?
It buried a genocide's worth of torsos in my yard,
It made extinct all species on the block.

Still I held him: buzz buzz woof woof—
Stirring again in my breast: ravishing but not redemptive

Night kept rising from the road.

He was the pesticide accumulating in the wax
He was the species of bee that encased its enemy in resin

In Somerset, 75 starlings fall dead from the sky; In Beebe, 5,000 crows.

That year we spent driving into Orion's belt—
That year—
            when I did not know where to put the dead man's body
so I had buried him here
in the back of my head,

pushing all his limbs down so he rested
there, in the curve of my skull.

We Navigate the River of Tar Under That Tethered Balloon of Light.

Listen: Failure's skin was a sheet
        stretched to be a screen, his skin
was the rough weight of canvas,
those things he showed me flickered
        on his flesh like a tide of luminescent fish,
like lapping tongues of fire, without
the images changing him. The trick
        to the screen is how often
it can be used by light, how
it takes in nothing of the picture
        (film leaving no film)
on his torso. I never learned
what projected those stories—if
        you could dissect him on a table,
would you find the apparatus? Some
halide lights in a row under the liver
        or two angler fish in his belly, each with an eye
turned towards a rib? Or did he pull
with some gravity or magnet the force
        of light or iron to him so that his tales
were mapped onto him like fleeting
tattoos? I learned to desire
        that jagged flick of shadows under his skin,
lay at night in motel beds
watching the ceiling, how
        the images cast up a cold residue
that looked like the surface
of gray water we slept beneath.

True North

He told me the story at a gas station closed for the night
The building a grayed-out white box

[light: diffuse, watery pools on the edges of the concrete floor]

His face burned by coals as a boy, he'd spent his youth
  searching for True North, always
a little closer, a little
further away

Researched Hausa: *It is with the body's water that one draws water from a well.*

Tried to get at it by pulling marks, scribbles from his hands—
  notations filling rooms of blackboards—
Built a boat on the shore for the floodwater to come and free—

      Chalk over the chalk, ghosting forms

I had been trying to do the dead man's work.

Had gathered, catalogued small animals from his land, labeled and
  frozen in bags
All the while trying to get at some clarity about the emptiness
He had left between the fallen bodies and the contaminated stream.

Failure read me Gould: *True north is not in a form. It is a shorthand for the suburb's*
  antithesis.

A threshold in the mind

Rowing, blood pools in the legs and lower torso

To reach it, you navigate by crow, releasing the bird from the ship
And following it—bird and then sails
Over the sea

To get towards an empty clarity

[the sea turning red and burning ships glowing gold and crimson in the
    night sky]

We sat in the car. I listened intently.

As he spoke, the sea rose on his skin.

[a same strange ambition burned within me to endure the same privation]

[fish that freeze without dying, sea creatures living at temperatures above
    boiling]

But never arrive, just go from country to country, find calm spots in the sea,
    always turning

At his closest, Failure taught Siberian tribes to recognize they had two selves:
        One self that moved through the village and lived,
        One self in an icy underworld

[police sirens lap at the edge of the gas station, blue light echoing back]

A well towards which we drove

[debris from the far-off disaster finally begins to wash against the shore]

Two worlds at once and a self in an icy underworld.

Using a Fleshing Machine

Failure took to building miniatures—
carving from soap bars first barges,
then on their backs, the spines
of skyscrapers, factories, railroads,
and airports. On some bars, a military
in formation. In others, industrial complexes
with tiny boardrooms. By the end of a month
his sculptures were so detailed, so resonant
with form that when we bent so our eyes
were level with the water, we could watch
them be launched—an armada of empire—
slowly exiting the horizon of sight. We would
stay there, hunched, until the ships began to dissolve
and sink—a whole fleet of capitalism in soap scum
at the bottom of the tubs and pools of every motel
from here to Reno.

Tanks of Fluid Converted to Motion

Land formed by fire—he pointed out mountains broken by lava,
fields laid by volcanoes, explained my home.

We joined the wandering population.

Red molten sulfur in the yellow tar sands.
Obsidian beneath the ground.

Out the window: glass framed by glass.
Failure reads the paper left behind at the restaurant, checks the stock quotes.

Salt flats exhibit the failure of water to remain,
Signs: the failure of the dust storm to abrade everything.

Exit 241 Burning fields—smoke over tar

Exit 629 Horses with hanging bellies

Exit 31 Pieces of torn tire / black birds flapping

I tried to untie to unyoke myself from human things,
To transcend.

Town after town named after dry riverbeds.
A sky as bright and hard as mica.

I wish on the first truck that passes: *Load of hay, load of hay, make a wish then turn away.*

I wish on the second truck. By the tenth truck,
I am done with wishing.

But also, it might be a sign,
wishes coming towards me, always in red, boundless.

Around the globe, snowpacks melt, the Nile dries, glaciers continue their
    slow retreat.

Color-blocked train cars, faded to the shades

of old Russian saints, Renaissance paintings
in perpetual motion beside us.

Bowl of sky,   hold my restlessness.

We Visit Every Nursing Home from
Amarillo to Yuma

Seek the litter of bodies.

Failure howls in a corner: Up and down the corridors from their rooms and
    wheelchairs
the elderly join in like a pack of dogs.

Failure pulls the moon into the surgical theater, spotlights the organs
    huddled together.

Their bodies keen to the light.
Failure chases medicine carts like rabbits down the linoleum.

The limbless prowl and wheel.
An unmoored language around us,
Each sunken chin rolling around a consonant.

Flesh closes over the scars. What remains
Compensates with lazy circles.

Failure smudges changes
Across their faces, Failure steals their teeth, hands out
Used dentures on the street. I take one that I knew.

When I chew, I chew twice, with my mouth and with my aunt's:
My teeth bite her teeth. My legs kick her amputated stumps.

-- -- --

Failure talks to me of the man I loved like a gangrenous limb
I tried to keep. He says in bed at night the memory stinks.

We scatter rock salt over motel hallways and beds. Grow nothing.
Every night, he saws the man off me and the stench subsides.

Failure predicts the phantom pain which comes like a needle traced
On the femur so the sawed-off limb plays a radio voice.

Like phonographs—Failure rotates the joint, reading out its cracks.

It sings itself out of, to me in the night. I wake
Each morning with the limb reattached.

I shove the dentures in my mouth and eat the breakfast meat.

What can you keep of the past but this?
I pile the dead idea of him back in, I get in the car and we go.

As It Appears Underneath a Cloud, Failure & I Drive Towards the Underbelly of the Sun

Network of highways punctuated by meat.

Carrion, roadkill illustrating the truth that all flesh
is one—fox indistinguishable from coyote from rabbit,
armadillo from dog from doe,
except by size, by spread of decay.

Road as memento mori.

Also, discarded sheets and single shoes at regular
intervals, inviting crime labs, inventions of the loss tale.

Failure reads Thoreau on animals: *They are all beasts
of burden in a sense, made to carry some portion of our thoughts.*

Failure reads me the *Odyssey* in translation as I work
the stick shift, the cruise control—
catalogue of birds as forms of gods or augurs:
gods' thoughts, made winged, stippled and in motion.

Outside, the bird arcs here are just a function
of speed and landscape, message we create
with our movement through space—

Only an expert could render it.

Failure flickers through the car and mimics—hawk beside me,
angry swan, indigo bunting, swallow spitting mud against the roof
    to make a nest;

Becomes: mineral crystals in the migrating head, pulled to magnetic fields.
Becomes: identical impulse in the prairie dog and guinea fowl to run.

Failure makes flawed creatures, undergoes the necessary trial of compassion
    to expand the self,

Pastures scurry by the windows.

Failure hits the car like a giant tumbleweed, breaking instantly
Into tiny pieces, leaving tiny marks.

Like Dostoyevsky, he casts our fears into the bodies of wild boars,
watches them rush over the cliff:

the moment of being driven
out of one's sense—a state
of displacement on the landscape—

Ecstasy. Close scene. Darkness descends.

Courting Manual for Failure

We brought you bouquets of flowering amoebas, filled florist shops with thawing tissue samples.

We wrote you poetry in genetic codes—ACCA GTTG ACG TCG—sonnets that albinoed the horses and stripped bare the swans.

We laced ourselves into corsets that broke ribs, suffocated organs, lungs, prolapsed the uterus.

We wore shoes to wear our bones to bunions, hose to record what we snagged against.

We have followed the rules of your law and your laws have led us here.

We delivered our animals to be sacrificed on metal tables, in the holy white-coated arms in hopes you'd favor us.

That fire we left burning for you in Centralia as a remembrance? That fountain of toxins we left you in the Hudson River to give you perpetually stilled fish to feed upon?

We gave you swathes of trailer parks made metal tinder and splinter, we hid under the force of your whine.

We have praised you publicly in our markets.

We have held you privately in our mouths with the cold barrel.

We build you ships and cast them into the sky and into the sea for you to break spectacularly down. We court you with the bouquet of iron wreckage. We court you with the decay of the rotting hulls.

Those peonies tissued in the field with grasshoppers, those violent and rising seas. We spread plagues around the world in planes, melt glaciers to give you a better view.

And you? You turn from us—the erotic flash
of the back of your neck, remembered fever of your hands on our haunches.

How Failure Dresses for Me:

We pass the deer, neck thrown
back from force of the fall, gullet
all the way open as if drinking
something in with death—world
in its final form, circumference. Failure took in
all of it, gathered, made from bits
of animal a moving coat, Jacob in death; imagine
a lover so, covered in carrion to meet you—honest
blood cast off—desire not to waste—did I mention
rotting? But beautiful—the animals shining and shivering
in motion, the sheen of hides filled with rags and cotton,
sewn and stretched, salted and sculpted, with
electrodes he implanted in a jaw or thigh
so that, once and whole beside me, a head or leg freed
and moving as if again from those original impulses
following the spark from the mind to the hoof from the hoof to the maw.

Failure Moves Through the Wolf's Hide;
as Death, Covers the Boat

Rather than caress the tender long limbs of you,

                                        we send

your man Shackleton not to war but to

                        a cold static drift on a solid sea.

A man must shape himself to a new mark directly

                                the old one goes to ground

With the Weddell Sea,

              we unman the vessel.

Failure lay back in the boat

                      on his fur coat, lay back on the pinions

of wings melting—the strap that held them

                                  to his forearm and biceps.

The leather strap strained and tied against the flesh.

                         He muscles his way under the boats.

While Shackleton rows . . . he pours one, two whiskeys,

                    he pours out one or two buckets of water.

If time will kill them anyway, kill them

                slowly and with the long low lights of seal blubber

      with the smoke inhaled under the cured canvas "thawed over a fire of
blubber" that covered the *James Caird*.

We had pierced the veneer of outside things

                We had seen God in His splendours,

                          heard the text that renders

"the corrugated surface of the frozen sea itself"   "a chaos of crumpled ice"

We shoot the last of the dogs with no ceremony. Even their tender
                                        flesh, no comfort to a body.

Read by lamps fashioned from sardine tins, bits of surgical bandages for wicks:

> *The war is not over. Millions are being killed.*
> *Europe is mad. The world is mad.*

The news being delivered again from the onion-thin pages

        In the grip of claustrophobia, one longs for the infinite.

Screws from the ship attached to their boots
                                to catch fire at a vision of the ice

"We had pierced the veneer . . . we had *heard the text that renders*"

Who called these men here to fight?
                I did and told them they would not return. Who paid these men
to test the limits of their flesh?
                        I did and told them the wages

Were poor. Who gave what of himself is best?
                                The man who found
The deepest contentment in his desolation.

After hoarding animals, Failure unleashes
                        the flocks of Shackleton's dogs across the ice.

The water table rises,
                we are stuck under the oilskin of the sea.

He was Failure's favorite

                    Misshapen son

Before coming up on land he announces

                                I am Shackleton

and the man ready to recognize the long dead greets him.

Winter

A huddle of buzzards over the blood

Circles burning the field, smoke rising on Christmas Day into the gray skies
A huddle of kindling, a huddle of birds

The horse loosed in the junkyard—brown haunches on the animal and
    wrecked cars

In deer season
Rib cages on the shoulder
Of the road like highway markers

In winter grass goes gray like silver, gray like ash

Drought kills trees in streaks of red across the hills

We planned to cut the mud into blocks to build a house, digging our home
    from the earth into a structure

Totem of stacked wheels, patterns carved into the rubber
American Talc Co. with its piles of stone and dust

Flayed yellow tumbleweeds drifted into banks against barbed-wire fences

American Talc turning the desert into dust people can cover themselves with
in the cities, a sheen of wildness in the ladies' underarms, the athletes' groins

The hard plastic crescent of moon
Over the car dealership
Lit by spotlights, tethered and sinking

Birds stipple the hillside
Birds fly:

At the edges of our vision, many people gather and stare quietly into the sky

Failure Recounts His Time in the Pulpit

How he coaxed away crutches and hope

Sinewy phrases wrap and twist, his voice
booms and swoops:
My children [he says] number in the thousands,
the dodo bird, Cape lion, red gazelle,
the snow eagle, the ivory-billed woodpecker. Among birds alone
my fame is called down the halls of Galliformes with awe.

The hymn begins:
Let us engage on the pilgrimage of failure. Let us
meet and marry on our ways through the dirt. Let
us call and respond in the disappearing landscape,
let us be nothing but melancholy on the road to the sky.

We pass the collection plate, add passports,
savings bonds and handmade effigies, false teeth and
prosthetic limbs. We leave with the promise
of what comes when all is gone.

In the pew beside me a boy turns to tell me
Failure is the apotheosis—that in turn
the boy tries to make god of himself
by shedding clothing and dollars
that he travels to the desert and lays down deep
in the sun under plastic bags and near
the empty milk jugs and pants. When
the patrol finds him, he ducks his head
beneath their truncheons and prays.
When he is returned to his shack, he goes
with a bit of god in him. Empty, he is ready
to be filled with the blessings of Failure.
Dented and bruised, he is ready.

Hold and hush the world, rest
from the unceasing motion, Rest
from the formaldehyde action of hope.

Satisfied, Failure coos the memory out, makes of his body
hood then feather, arch then altar.

In re: Failure, Body Where Tar and Light Meet

Days without another body   even by sight   accumulating

I dreamed while he drove all night   that I had filled my ears with chalk dust
That I had burned my tongue like a cork to write with   I lay under a slate
While Failure wrote and erased it, wrote and erased it

One man learns to mine, another learns to blow things up

Where there should have been none, there were deserts of beach,
    cleared by storms

A heap forever, even a desolation, unto this day

From disaster movies, I can imagine anything
Crashing into anything

See in clouds—an organic approximation of a frozen bomb—
In soft wool, wire, tumbleweeds

The bomb that gravity lowered on Japan with quiet and characteristic indifference,
Thirty-two feet per second, per second

In a room full of heat, light turned on is experienced as heat
In a room full of dark, like a destroying fire

Burn oil from a whale, oil from a well

A desire through practice to find the body's true wildness

Machine That Leaves and Never Returns

Failure opens his coat, offers
me from his pockets the field behind
my father's house accidentally sown with onions or
the sun edging over the lip of the pool in summer,
grass tended by groundskeepers—

                                        and when I choose
the field, it disappears inside the bodies of the grasshoppers
and when I choose the pool, he fills the chlorine with carcasses of bees
and when he offers me arroyos, he sends angry horses through them,
flash floods, La Llorona catching the edge of my dress. I'd take the sky
full of birds but he snips their wings, lets the folded umbrellas of them fall,
500 at a time on Louisiana. I'd take the snow in ruts of the road
but there Failure stands, handing out contaminated soil
free to area residents, PCB-dredged silt. He opens the menagerie
to emphasize conquest, zoos for education, and lets the raw and mangy
bears be pelted with stones. From the way he offers me
the lake, the water will dry, the boats will fall to the bottom, dogs
will roll in the dead fish, until we curse whatever rubs up against us
down at the foot of the marriage bed, edged in roe.

Failure Dreams of Elements

A gun gives you the body, not the bird.
—HENRY DAVID THOREAU

Dream, Water: I slowly pull you through the water by a rope. In this dream, you are a corpse. In the river for days, you are bloated (skin taut like a balloon). The rope is around my waist. The mud clings to my shoes. In this dream, your corpse has been beneath the river for days, skin taut with water. The rope around my waist. Riverbed in my shoes. I keep trying to turn your face up, like rolling a kayak. Your corpse has been on the river for days. The river has made of you (your flesh) a boat. The waist-rope clings, your face to the sky, rolling.

Dream, Water: Rope strung over (across) the field. Fish after fish hung from clothespins by their tails. Slowly the sea pours out from them. The sea runs over their imbrication of scales. The sea plants itself in the field, (deep) in the earth.

Dream, Water: Levitates the assistant over water. So that *he can make the truth come out of her mouth.* Fish hook, fish hook, fish hook: a necklace.

Dream, Air: In which the buzzards crisscross the valley.

Dream (scatter): In which you are the tree.

Dream in which you are the warrior, buried in the earth.

Dream, Fire: Two burns on the chest where they pulled the soul back into the heart.

Dream, Fire: Coyotes scatter over the fields, chase down the wounded, eat.

Dream, Water: The book is sick and must be fed fishes.

Dream, Elements: The peat burns the field to ash, the ash distilled, in the room, you pour the whiskey into a glass.

Dream, Earth: In the mouth (underneath the tongue) of every body in the graveyard, the battlefield, you enclose an orange, lemon (pomegranate) seed.
      Year One: Grass covers everything.
      Year Two: A hundred sticks, small twigs to trip on.
      Year Three, Year Four: The roots tick open the jawbones.

Dream, Year Five: An orchard pouring from their mouths.

Project for a Machine for Grasping

Emergence is what arises from the body
struck in the sternum by the car bumper
wrenched behind the turbine, what arises
is death from the body, an emergency coaxed

out of it, as if the fly had laid its worm in the flesh
as if the accident writhed inside the marbled muscle until
the machine freed it. *While the brain shuts down,*
tiny people, tiny horses dance in the corner

of the eyelids, dogs jump over one another's
backs, elephants balance gently on that solid
knuckle of hoof. The act of severing lodges in the limb,
in the torn corner of the heart, in the cut that wears

down bone. Ambulances lazily circle the city. The silica settles
for years until one cough loosens it in the body; it begins
in the ambulance to fall back onto the world from the trees
where its dark snow has been settling. The ashy street

a week after the storm. Walking on the mounds, the backs
of buried houses and topsoil, the beta rays burrow
up through the body, through the cut foot, begin in mutation
to bloom out a new and legless body, emerge across

the red forest left behind. Failure roots, ruts, roams
through the body, scoping out the most dramatic entrance,
imagining his face emerging finally at the end
of the beautiful sequence of those flashing blue lights.

Partage: Dividing of the Spoils

On that seventh day, endless fire casting up images.

Lions covered in flies. Water where none was.

For a time God seemed a vast body, held against us, above us, edged in neon.

For a while we prayed.

Failure read of "birds red from the forge,"

17 tons of mercury released to the atmosphere,

And we saw the Corpse everywhere.

I pretended not to know him, though his face, his body had been etched
into me.

Though he was what I ran from.

On the side of the road, a man with his thumb out.

Who were we to turn down fate?

The rustles and murmurs of the world.

It could have been something sent down for us,

Lightly embalmed, with an animal's jaw strapped to his back.

Not one to turn away a stranger, Failure shoved the Corpse in the trunk for later.

Not one to let decay go unused, Failure strapped the Corpse to the hood
of the car.

The Agonizing Blue of the Sky

Billboards at flat and brutal angles to the road

From the speakers of the radio and the drive-thrus, ragged voices, dry rivers
    of sound across the land

I try to cultivate detachment

One hand out the window, cupped lightly in the sun

In the car, Failure recounts the Zone of Alienation, Ukraine (circa 1986),
    takes me through the errors he causes, lists lovingly: slips, lapses,
    mistakes, errors made in planning and in execution, of commission,
    of omission, designer errors, operator errors, errors from the outside,
    deficiencies in judgment—

A train beside us for the many miles of Texas,
in our vision for a hundred
Tumbleweeds between Infinitys and Accords

In our trunk, the body I'd said Kaddish for
for a year

Yellow ticks of the metronome forward, odometer counting out the miles
Hydraulic mines washing away the mountains

10,000 fish die above us in a Michigan lake.

I am telling you the only story there is

Of falling in and out of love concurrently
Of falling and rising concurrently

At the rest stop, Failure hunches with an X-Acto knife in the backseat

cuts from the Southwest anything not water or highway, so we are left

with the lace of passageway

With a vision of what might sustain us

I was there to bury the Corpse, I was there to drive the car.

Nocturne

At night I slept in the middle of the bed—
Failure would crook his knees into mine
and with my knees I'd push the Corpse's legs
into a bent position—Failure would encircle my waist
and I would throw my arm
around the waist of the Corpse
as if he were an accordion I'd strapped
onto my back—as if I stretched my arms
around his rib cage to begin to play.

Failure Tends to Fall

asleep at the wheel
        to the slight rocking
on the sea of macadam.
        To keep him
from this, to keep his eyes
        open I tell him stories
of the trip to Antarctica
        the Corpse and I did not make. I begin
with the vast claustrophobia
        of nothing in every direction,
how my eyes became attuned
        to the smallest jog of ice,
to the echo of seals
        under my feet, pulsating
against my ear
        when I lowered
my head to the ground.
        The air is as dry as a desert,
bones strewn above
        the immutable stark surface.
Corpse played a scientist
        studying an iceberg
bigger than this country:
        "If you want
to understand a view of God,
        then this is the scale
the infinite works on."
        Nothing grows
above the surface,
        even though
it's made of water, and so, and still,
        I hauled

six large branches
  of a tree
to plant there. I upended
  them, Failure, on the tundra
and buried them so that
  from a distance they appear
to be something
  that has died. I did it
solely to taunt the land.
  I did it to underscore God's waste.

Antarctica, Redux

Failure says his ancestors
have owned that property for years.
If you watch it, he says, you can see
their ideas moving beneath it,
releasing bit by bit the water into
the water.

Failure's Experiment with the Sea

In the motel corner, Failure knits with the tentacles of jellyfish,
he makes a net to cast into the sea to catch fish in; the genesis
of time he says starts in the belly and ascends. If they are
constantly in motion, they cannot be strewn on the beach
like glass insulators, like magnifying glasses, emptied
snow globes, sand underneath a bottle's end. Failure holds
one of the bodies up to the past and scries: he sees I was full

of you but transparent, like the air inside a plane moving
through air: lungs body hull sky. They kept
coming to the edge of the water and dying in the sand, were
not umbrellas or blooms—tiny citizens in exile, while beached
whales were kings. They populated the world of stinging things,
were kin to wasp and scorpion: one water, one air, one earth.

I kept carrying them back, covered in gloves and a raincoat,
I used buckets and tongs and baskets. I cast them out. But
the water kept pushing them towards me, nudging back
those translucent vessels, corpse and displacement of the sea.

I Tell Failure the True Story of the Corpse

For that half year I was so happy
I pulled down all the generators
all the telephone lines; long lanky summer
while we slowly became wire, I blew
out tires and candles, pushed drills
into derricks and fractured earth
to find the oil, ruined water and wells,
broke teeth and gears. And my happiness
like a bowling ball on a trampoline
pulled towards itself all
disaster—the great-aunts were
buried ten to a plot in the Independence
Cemetery, the uncles lit cigarettes outside
pulled smoke into tumors
while the snow stuck in their hair
and the spokes of their chairs, and
the junkyards filled with the wreck
of every car in town, and tap water
like lit torches gleamed with fire, and the wars
escalated and reaped bodies, cities, and
our love pulled into our bed the dissolution
of all marriages around us, so we
trailed behind our happiness (tin cans
tied with twine) all that
disappointment in our wake, broken ships
we towed between the icebergs
on our way down to the glaciers
of the pole.

In Return, Failure Tells Me Stories

1) Failure says to brake for the miniature horses, to grow one, to load the back of the pickup truck with tiny hooves. Failure wishes to start a near-failing farm, place to raise ostrich, buffalo, and emu. Place to graft pecan trees and to practice graft. Roulette wheel spinning. Suitcases with money and seeds, government grants.

2) I fall asleep while Failure name drops: Dionysius, Orpheus, Aeneas, Longfellow's wife burned in her dress, Custer, Gandhi, MLK, Nietzsche kicked by a horse, Mozart with his crippled hands, Marie Curie, Hitler the painter but not Hitler the leader, Picasso the son not Picasso the painter, Audubon's mother whose monkey killed his first parrot.

3) He lists what he stole in the Great Strike, looting freight cars for: *Corn in sacks, cotton in bales, wool in bags, bread, crackers, fruit, sugar candies and confectionaries, hides, leathers, shoes, queen's ware, glassware, clothing, hay, whisky, alcohol, tobacco, coal, coke, silks, jewelry, even assorted volumes of* Chambers's Encyclopaedia *and a number of Bibles.*

4) Failure thigh-deep in the field of wheat, head cocked back for the gunshot—the house, every window lit, deep in the midday sun. Failure offers one palm to each black dog circling the chair while the master knotted and swinging says nothing. Failure starves alongside the man, feels the same hurt, weakness, headache, dizziness, nausea, terrible aches in the joints. Soon they both wander in the hallucinations of weightlessness.

5) What souvenirs he buys and what he keeps in the glove box: Rattlesnake eggs, pickled eggs, pickled pig's feet, many things in jars, moccasins, state spoons, tarnished spurs, rugs, zoos animated in pictures, diseases and guns, beavers turned into felt top hats, whales made lamp oil for parlors and bones for corset, buffalo made into factory belts.

6) His hero story: Failure against obstacles delivers a man finally to his destination—badly, half driven mad by sorrow—fires burning offstage in buildings, the old, boring site of apocalypse, leaves him sitting in a rocking chair while he drives off to begin soda-ash mining, to open the store for tourist info, prospecting tools, postcards, and Western hats.

Annotated Plans for an Evacuation

Traveling past billboards, treeless marsh, unpaved roads
the parking lot, the supermarket, the highway

The Corpse naps on my shoulder.

In the dream, growing seasons shorten, torrential rain & flooding, cattle die
    in the ice-covered pastures.

Meanwhile, we pass The Stay Inn, The Landing Strip, Heartbreak Shack.
El Paso—Non-Stop Beautiful Ladies.

Carrying rice, frozen meat, engine parts, pass
distant steam vents in the bare land
the weed that takes over the telephone pole, submerges the house.

Illusion of water—mirage or tar—
                      loose gravel slapping pebbles.

We blah blah blah.

As far as I could tell the Corpse had no dark soil inside him
        Did not pulse   Did not breathe
would eat with disdain, boredom,
if we worked his jaws and gullet.

If at rest, rested. If in motion, moved,
herky-jerky like a stuttering record, a flapping film, a torn sign on the road.

Armadillos at night, shadows of itself the road throws up.

We pass endless electromagnetic waves: X-ray machines, tanning booths,
    power lines, radio antennae, video display terminals—tiny pulsating
    oceans we drive through.

*I barter with Failure for his extinction: I'll fill the bee box with pesticide just to watch you open
    the catch, pour in the burning oil—just help me find a way to lay him down.*

Over the man's slack mouth
                        the bare bulb of the moon swings on its black cord.

The child rides the bike in endless circles
                        around the drained pool of the motel court.

Project for a Machine for the End of Civilization

By day we drive and by night
we sleep and fuck. In that order. Not
in that order. We argue:
Should we keep the Corpse
in a cooler or a valise?
Does he need dry ice? Should he sleep
in the bathtub, bed, or car?
Like having a small child or dog whom Failure
wants to teach tricks to, convinced
as he is that the neurons still hold motion and pattern
after death. On Sunday, we lower the body in honey
as a balm—on Monday we bathe the flesh and cover him
in pollen for bees who come and crown him
with their golden motion. We apply
arsenic crystals to his wrists and temples.
By day we drive, by night we rest.
We fill and empty the gas tank
as if we were the twin aortas of our car's heart.
We pump like ventricles. Tracing the branches
of our driving, the forced returns, the long
straightaways would feel to the hand like sketching out
the causeways of a body. Something then. Each morning
I decide to put all the faith I have in motion. We drive
and sleep and fuck. Each day I become less of a person—
A single bird along the bare ruined highway.
My fingers rubbed raw from recording, from
the sense of something approaching.
We drive down the road towards it like fire
running down a fuse.

Failure's Dream

After Laurie Sheck

Failure pulls the cosmonaut close, kisses his cold lips, kisses his lips from
    space, lolls around his tongue in the man's mouth.

I run alongside the car beside the soldiers, trying to hand the cosmonaut a
    bouquet I have made him filled with roses from wire and tissue paper.

First Failure kisses him, then Khrushchev pulls the man in close, so close
    he seems almost to nuzzle the nape, almost to be inhaling the tar where
    they sealed the neck of his spacesuit.

With the hundred history books, I riffle the pages to make birds. I fold the
    facts into boats and launch them over the Aegean Sea.

Failure teaches the students to worship the Gipper, renames the wars inside
    the country, lauds the mayor's decision to burn down the town rather
    than let the bricks fall to his far-off enemy.

Before he kisses me, the cosmonaut admits entering the capsule again
    was the saddest moment of his life. Even at the table, you can see him,
    tethered by a rope in that infinite space.

Failure locks the hatch and stands outside the ship, waving, waving,
    waving to the small face that recedes through the stars all the way
    down to earth.

Every Day a New Pair of Sunglasses,
Every Day a New Hat.

Failure poses in front of the giant plastic alien, the giant plastic Uncle Sam,
    the tepee, the mesa. While the camera may render him indistinct, in
    each shot the expression is clear.

As if I'd shone a flashlight through his body and inside:
against a wall, writhing, shadow puppets—
too many animals for the pen to hold.

I'd once used my grandmother's ruby glass to cast red onto everything: Bowl
    with a heart. TV with a heart—Everything ready to beat.

In my mouth the glass vial of mercury to measure
the heat of my blood.
My teeth against it, ready to bite, resisting.

Outside us, the edges of the desert orchards. The trees are envelopes of
    yellow leaves, tied in the country song, here or there a leaf edged in the
    black of the burning sun.

When Failure talks, he hits his open hand against his breastbone
for emphasis, as if his body might disappear
in its projections, its own murky insides, his experiments.

Like autumn, the world burns through what is living, ashes the rest on the
    dry ground.

Failure Names the Babies

Knuckles Sing in the Night. Cries by the Window.
Prayers Explode Cheap Candles in Church. Wears Away
In Routine. Carrier of Plague to a City. Lost Mail.
On the Pyre of the Trailer. Train Whistle Never Leaves.

Thief. Procrastinator. Orphan. One (Only) Perfect Morning.
TV Smile. Skins the Rabbits. Nine-Month Process. Whetstone.

Kicked to the Curb. National Holiday.
Microscope. Souvenir of the Morgue. Hindsight.
Good Woman in a Bad Position. Bad Man
in a Good Position. Child Between. Antibody.

Microlending Scandal. Hoof and Mouth. Volatile Rain
On Baked Soil. Truck Route. Declaration. Armed Zone.

Hospice. Cracked Nuclear Core. Where Were You?
High-Profile Investment. One-Off. Crackshot.
Extortion. Mass Bird Death. Tsunami Redux.
Formaldehyde. ELE. Preservative of Grief.

Failure on the Theme of the Ruined Landscape:

Imagine up one wall of the deserted airplane hangar
    A hundred glass terrines, waiting for the dioramas he'd collected. As he talked
        about the quarry, jagged rock flashed

across his skin, sulfured water rose up
    his flesh. *Active granite section, abandoned*
        granite section. Mines with stepped sides, pyramids,

making of the world an abstract sculpture, drilled perfect holes
    in the side of rocks, exact geometry
        amid chaos. Or when he pointed to the rusted

hulls, all around, we saw footprints
    of a hundred workers and heard the clang
        of their tools over the sand, over the sea. The timber

felled across hills like the punched-down grass of bodies
    writhing to make a place in it to sleep.
        He kissed me and traced

with an index finger across my back
    the path the rail made
        in the mountain, and I was then

jagged and marked by the low scream
    of the train around my waist. Tops of mountains
        lopped off, *escarpment, ridgeline*, arcing and angular,

felled by dynamite. A scaffolding fourteen stories high and rebar
    in the concrete jutting like twigs of a nest, like reeds
        swaying in the grass, the forklifts gathered in a bunch of stems.

Cars in their mass, pauper's graves, bathers in polluted waters,
    men diving into filth with abandon. The canvas of the ship's
        decay (like tattered flags, flapping) rose above me.

We hunkered down
    in the piles of trash, in the valleys cleared for the dam,
        in the low dark landscape of coal.

Inco tailings, nickel tailings, uranium tailings,
    Trees burned from the inside out like chemo through a body.
        The derricks in herds across the landscape grazed dry.

He turned to each action slowly
    called it up through the boundless earth,
        then caulked it to his skin, just as a carbon rod stroked

with fur produces static electricity, he projected on the lit walls
    of the hangar and I saw the slideshow: History
        of the ruin we made of the land and a chronicle

as we disappeared of the ruin becoming sublime.

An Emaciated Horse Led by His Master

Wrestle through the illness, through the body of

Proteus though he be made of burning fire

Though Failure be beast or wild bird

Though he score your face with claws, though

He pinions you under the heavy weight of a shoulder's flesh

Burrow in the dank dark fur and whelp

In the common speech of the body, no passage,

In the sound of the voice keeping silence, praise,

At the extremity of the translucent ion, the body holds

for I had placed myself behind my own back refusing to see myself

Slight weeping, I was told hold still, hold on

While he shifts from mammoth to ostrich, razorback to jackdaw,

Is the face is the body still there while

He bites your calves with the fangs of a snake while

One after the other then side by side he tends

The seals that nudge your ankles, those seals

That push and hold your flesh down in tide,

Herds of muscle, sleek for the ocean, body tumbled between the fur and fur

And so as my body gave up, I became

What I was; I ceased to be what I was not.

When you settle on your own face, let's both be done with you.

Agriculture Begins:

Cleared forests and carbon for warmth
Rice in paddies and cows in pastures and the methane rising—

Failure evinces in the boy a tenderness towards the pig,
A need to kiss its soft ears and mouth.

And the family sleeps by the rotten grain,
And the workers breathe in the wasted cotton, the boles.

Pause for the Black Death, as plows and shovels still, the world temporarily
    cools—

The gods made land so we could bury in it—

From coal, release the old sunlight it holds and build again.

***

We till the fields and tend the fruit.

Bacon called the self "a grinding machine":
One machine causes dreams of horses, another great sadness.

Returning, like Persephone,
To the scene of the crime, willingly, repeatedly.
I plant my body in the ground and in the spring I grow.

Like fire that burns the field, prepares it for crops, let the mind be seared by
    failure into readiness.

Smaller rabbits this year, fewer quail—

At last the animals starved by drought will eat the cactus, spines and all.

***

[crops that dissolved into earth with drought, crops that through mouths
became winged things and flew, ice that wilted the lettuce, train car that
stalled on tracks, water diverted to the city, that we had no wood for coffins,
that I could keep no hens alive, that leaves become lace overnight, the field
a gown with delicate feathers, mold that ruins the hay, in your lungs the
blooms, in your lungs the delicate tendrils and trees from the mines]

***

Trees burned back to root. The long-drawn-out filaments of smoke.
    Saltbrush that chokes everything.

Egyptians covered mummies in wet linen to plant corn on,
Osiris sprouting green, flowers through the cloth.

Woodpeckers work to hollow the flesh of the tree.

Ten years of growth, ten years of fire.
The worst fire in the worst drought
of recorded history.

[Cue: Each year, a new state's announcer speaks this line.]

[Plant upon your gods, make them fields and keepers of the fields, if crops
fail on the bodies of gods you have proof of earth acting upon you, proof of
the sun's vast power, proof of indifference and decay.]

—A scourge over the sky of birds and white ashy snow.

Ancestors in the ground means you own the land.

A slow combing through the dark warm soil—

Each year, we bury more of it.

Failure Burns the Taxidermy Museum

Bear splayed open   Zebra with two jaws   Horse's back charred as if with a saddle

Deer,   elk,   oryx,   ibex   //   Turkey,   fox,   bison,   boar

Broke bones, twisted animal   into something recognizable   Made a scene   of death

Salt the hides before mounted   Enter the Open Mouth Division   of the championships

Buffalo,   weasel,   bobcat,   jackdaw   //   Cougar,   antelope,   Barbary sheep

Failure time-lapse videos   flies & maggots   Corpse: whole then spread   as bone

against the ground,   Failure as woven   of worms, not silkworms   a garment, clods

of dust,   roots from his shoulders He walks in it to   and fro upon the earth,

he walks up and down the runway and the plank   Inside casing,   a broken

smoking mirror of wings   Covered with the distant   silence of the fields—

Javelina,   eagle,   cape-tanned coyote,   /-/ Sea mink,   bush wren,   razor-backed boar

If he could,   he'd make with tissue: nerves along the strand of seaweed,   hand

from a possum's stomach,   corneas in the starfish,   kidneys among the squids' tentacles,

intestines from   the vulture   who ate Prometheus   Antidote, anecdote   //   giant shrike,

hoopoe   Later, to console himself,   Failure remakes a creature,   saws sews limbs

together and hooks   the beast to our car battery   to make it live   They are fleeting, these

bobcats and deer,   these shrews and vultures   but the hour or two   in which they

dance and ask questions of the world cheers him   stockpiles in him   a brave and generous passion

Fecundity, Expanse

Dregs in the hotel glasses, arranged in lines of song.
Skin cells on tub bottoms, my hair
on the brush, tangled in the trash, curled in the drain.
All day, he touched bodies and objects—fingerprints
on doorknobs, windowsills, and coins—obsessed
with the outside of gloves, books, crepe paper,
anything that could be bloated or ruined with water. We remade
the world in residue. I lived inside the constant pulsing
of my absent home, *an uncommon and ever-present idea*
of the recalled native land in the mind. When we stop,
I lie down in tall grass to form a silhouette.
When we stop, I lie for a long time in the edge of waves
until my body has been carved into beach. I leave my body
in the beach *so it fills and empties.* We made effigies
in ice, in weeds woven in grass, in peonies floating. When we began
to sleep together—in a desultory manner at first
and then with great urgency, I let his come
leak out of me purposefully, with art
so that sometimes I left behind
a spot, sometimes a crescent, a harvest scythe.
I let the stains wax and wane with the month, the moon;
Every fourth week, the story bled.
Had you read our motel beds across,
like a comic strip, you would have seen us
making with our bodies a calendar,
situating ourselves physically inside a narrative of those days.

The Learned World, the Conversable World

Failure: plays the part of our baggage, esp. our leather steamer trunk, with two inexplicably rusty nails in front

Corpse: plays the part of a porcelain doll, human-sized, hair comprising twigs—hard to carry, prickly & fragile—bleeds from chopped off pieces, must have read Dante

I: plays the part of self, loads Failure & the body in and out of car, crosses state lines, gambles away gas money

The opacity of our lives to each other kept us yoked together.

Failure: plays the hummingbird, metallic whirr from something organic

I: the grappling hooks, punctured tire of the wheelbarrow, soaked matchbox, creosote through the windows, gasoline on the floorboards

For dinner, Corpse: plays the phonograph, which he calls Hour of Performance from the Long Dead

Failure: plays the Turin Shroud in exhibition, first instance of photography, his mark on a man bathed in desiccant

I: the great ocean of prairie, unfathomable instrument of the insect's legs, pilgrimage

We send everything we find east for the exhibition. People of the screen not people of the book.

Failure: plays the tourist-photographer trying to capture the church—a branch always in the way, autofocus fail

Corpse: plays the subject in the photo—accidental tree from out of his heart, tree from out of his jaw

Anselm Kiefer: A rain of ash, coal, straw, and burnt cardboard

Corpse: plays the stadium lights: powder-coated die-cast tempered flat glass lens

Failure: plays thieves digging at the grave of Charlie Chaplin. When he has been made risen, one man puts his fingers to Charlie's cheek. One does the ghost of the tramp.

Failure fast-forwards: unanswered ransom for Chaplin's corpse. Jail.

Ezra Pound: *And the living were made of cardboard*

Failure: plays the first Emperor of China, standardizes arrows so a dead soldier's arsenal stays dangerous

I: play one man hanging from a nail, one man with a goat's bell around his neck, one man bird-dogged to the ground

Corpse: in mass production, standardizes the holes made in a man, feathers that rise from his skin like splayed wings

I: play transhumance, the seasonal migration of livestock, the movement into a felled man's arms

Failure says: Why hang on to this love? Why keep something deep and fatal beside you?

The Failure of Sequestration

We made, between us, waste.
      When our love died—bedded salt formations,
      when our love leached back in, salt caverns and domes.

I store the radioactivity of the Corpse in me, its half-life
      decaying in transit across state lines. Watch
      the critical pathway from air to pasture, from pasture

to cows to milk—I absorb the Corpse in the organs or tissue.
      A crumpled flower. A rain-drenched parade and sashes.
      Storage is by definition an interim measure.

I ran the risk of what might be called human scenarios. Each led
      to a saturated zone, a plume, water or airborne events.
      A brain whose synapses will fire until they're ash.

To make of him
      a barren solution,
      a basalt volcanic lava, to cast him

in clay made from the mountain's ash. When the Corpse was alive,
      I covered every surface of him
      with silt to reduce the particles we breathed. Still

in the air, the surface water—resuspended by wind, by fire
      from the beds of rivers, lakes, or seas until the fish
      are poisonous, the trunks decay.

Mutations accumulate. Feathers turn, then
      the curve of beaks, feet made webbed
      then spindly, bones start to crack when flying,

feathers absorb tar and finally flightless
    land-driven birds limp
    across the forest floor to underground homes.

Small doses of radiation linger—here at the cherry's core,
    in the mushroom, in the heart
    and liver of the wild game.

Baptize the Long-Dead

If Failure the doctor walks the corridors, my love, and laughs, I sleep curled
    with the Corpse on a hospital bed waiting. The Corpse packs his bags for
    the delivery, the Corpse falls down on the freshly mopped floor.

If the body peels like an onion back, the door will not open, if the blood
    half-digested cools.

Against my window rains the detritus kicked up by the mower
from the Corpse they remove the detritus left by death: organs and viscera,
    corneas, etc.

The hospital refashions itself,
maps the migration of the germs from body to body.

Failure pockets syringes and the night crews wash the remaining needles in
    a dirty bucket.

If the condition of being is characterized by a silence, if the god room is
    empty—frequent perturbation of the soul—if the messengers are half-
    beast half-bird, if half-bird half-man, if the hybrid now and then—

Corpse: "I do not sleep though I sometimes doze off a little. If up, I am talked
    to and in my efforts to answer cause pain."

The taxidermist refashions what can't be preserved
(ears, eyes, nose, lips, and tongue—parts we make a sensory life out of)

Corpse: "The fact is I think I am a verb instead of a personal pronoun."

An infection of sight—

Like the Greeks, we pour broth into his moldering jaws.

Failure's Beatitudes

Blessed are the plastic rings that hold cans
Blessed the logs in a gas fireplace
Blessed the landfall, blessed the landfill
He quivers in pleasure at the approach of illness, fatigue, miasma
He quivers in sight when I watch him
Blessed are Failure's early days on the farm, the always-ragged crop, sick
    cattle with their sores and distended bladders
Blessed are the tree's boles, its pusses and excrescences
Blessed the bench seats in a yard, the broken lawn chairs and discarded bottles
Blessed the fake flowers and knockoff purse
Blessed are the sheep that proceed from Dolly
Blessed are the bones in the catacombs of the Natural History Museum,
    those extinct birds and beasts, those blights of early jostling
Blessed the early artificial heart that crushes blood, calf heart in the torso
Blessed the littered, unexploded shells in the field
Blessed the tailings from pulp and paper mills
For the brilliant green of the hills, he gives me the deep brown when the sea
    has risen and retreated across its soil
Blessed the empty pews, burned out bulbs in the electric prayer candles
Blessed the Little Ice Age, walking across cold rivers—boats frozen at dock,
    fish underneath layers of milky glass
Blessed the ruined and stained robes, edged in brocade, the plasticized
    cherubs, the marble painted to look like marble
Blessed be the bison, the passenger pigeon, blessed the men and women who
    painted the demolished dioramas, then the movie sets
Blessed the glaciers that razed the villages
Blessed the brackish estuary, brown with silt, the free-floating product plume
Blessed the photographer's "meaningless blur, grain, muddy exposure,
    drunken horizons and general sloppiness"
Blessed the ring of people staring inward, at the catastrophe
Blessed the whole failing project of sight

Failure & I Decide What to Do with the Body

Failure inflates the Corpse and ties it to my wrist
with a long red ribbon like a dirigible which hits
the ceiling or doorways whenever I move. Failure shrinks
and taxidermies the Corpse like a small fawn. We make a hundred
versions of him from meat we buy in the market
float him in the Dead Sea until he's brined
then roast him in the fire and feast.
At night we lie under the stars
and if the ground's too coarse,
we lean our heads against the Corpse, his belly and his haunches.
At night we prop him against our motel door with a sombrero as a warning
    to strangers,
or we hang him on a tree or we use the angles of his body
to create a court's width of chalk outlines inside of which we play the
    murder game.
While we drive we play the car game—what to do with the Corpse:
and every time we open the trunk he is there, bound,
and every time I open my suitcase, he is there, sleeping—valise, reincarnated.
They turn me into a list-making machine—I tally and account.
To play hide-and-seek, we ensconce the body in a cubicle
and then every wardrobe box and landfill fridge.
We plant the Corpse inside each carcass we find on the ground
to quiet his movement. Still, no matter the permutations
of the day, I wake to his body in the night, silent and cold beside me.

On Set: The West

Place for the inner restlessness in the deep sky. Sand pushing a way
into you, at the corners of your eyes, edges
of the windows and vents. Dust to dust, shack

to ghost town. Flat front of stage sets.
Reenactment of Little Bighorn, reenactment of Custer's Last Stand.

Failure plays the Mr. who carries the bullets, small pellets
of death and smoke, bony stars on his heels, reins in the hand,
calluses numb to their motion.

Were we still at night we'd hear
the tender, lonely howls. Might catch the gray edge
of a coyote running.

Truckers herd their products across the expanse of roads tars plains,
wrangling lettuce microprocessors plastic dolls past
barbed-wire fences, gathering monsoons, cops lazy behind the brush coiled
to strike—into the corral of delivery docks the loading ramps—men push

boxes up on silver wheels into the warehouse where they slice
cardboard apart and trim the packaging away
like men in an abattoir—

the smell of Stryofoam lifting briefly from their uniforms.

At the motel, I rest on cracked lawn furniture, order drinks from a waiter
    who keeps receding
halfway between me and the bar,

infinitely into the distance.

Failure tans in radiation beds of atomic blasts, sits with clothes tattered by
    bullets—

A dark continental vastness stretches ahead of us.

Failure's hands are edged in fur when he turns the radio
from station to station, from static to static.

We Prepare for the Coming Blackouts

I compile weather reports
We work to conduct electricity
Slowly build in a field a mound of glass insulators, a line
Of water jugs through which we'd send current sent by the sky
Outside the motel rooms, all summer, flashes of music
Car radios tracing out the edges of highway
A forlorn mechanical feeling
The transformers and lines can't cool
This heat is a harbinger of heat
Ransack the ocean—In the sea, diaphanous
Clouds of membrane, without eyes, stomach, face, or spine
I had been living with that old feeling of erasing myself
From the days between this and some other event
Hopped-up Greyhounds sleek in heat
Empty train beds, burned apex of the motel roof—

Deforestation and a quietly fleeing universe
Failure tracks his movements through the extinctions
The animals attack, bite, wound, and worry each other
Fire licks up the telephone pole, burns its shadow onto brick
Each history told different losses
The joint, the choir invisible
Watch night black cloud of coming storm through windows
Baked hay, baked cardboard, baked signs, baked cars
We give the Corpse Vicodin to still
The coming silence, to wake him from the fugue state
We wrap his wrists and metacarpals for the wrestling ring
The Swenson Fire, The Rockhouse Fire, The Canyon Complex Fire, The
    White Hat Fire

Windmills, fencing for rodeos, horse pens; girders and giant winches

Smoke reflected in the black oil, tar of the road

Here the vultures eat even the bones of the baby calf

Leave just the pelvis, a single hoof

Gutted-out buildings and gun galleries

Heat waves shimmer over the dried-out lakes, the dormant volcanoes

The Deaton Cole Fire, The Iron Mountain Fire, The Possum Kingdom
    County Complex Fire

Of the far-flinging darkness, sing to me

As the blackout rolls towards us

We go inside the abandoned bunker

To greet the light

Interview, Recto

What was your childhood like?

Like many, it began in a well.

Had you fallen?

Yes, like an inadvertent wish, then the rain of others' desires came down upon me.

When was your first transformation?

I could not keep my mother happy, nor could I keep her body. I lived between my desire to stop her suffering and my desire to stop being her suffering. I lived between wanting her to stay forever and wanting what time would do to her. One of these wishes turned me into a wolf, one into a rabbit. I lived inside the fur and the fur.

How often do you run away?

There are records.

Have you read them?

I find it best not to know what others think of me. I destroy mirrors.

Why did you choose this speaker?

She was lovely and foolish in her desire to be good. Also I knew what would happen to her.

Who are your enemies?

Time undoes me in the most mundane ways—and death. You may not realize, I am actually quite weak. I have asthma and my ideas are hardly ever patented. I have invested in a thousand schemes gone wrong.

Whom have you loved chiefly?

The metronome, the subway, the cartographer, the skins of animals Shackleton's men hid in.

Whom have you studied under?

Oh, rust—weeds, decay. All the great suicides—ambition in its usual forms—taxes & revolutions & inventions. Mainly my parents and how each failed in their own particular effortless way. The master who passed on to me his conjuring skills, my own dear heart that recedes.

Interview (Verso)

What was your childhood like?
   Like many, it began in the sea.

Had you fallen?
   Yes, while swarms of immortal jellyfish spread over the earth. I packed myself in a weakened salt.

When was your first transformation?
   The surgeons in Russia removing a fir sapling from a man's lung? It was then I knew I could go anywhere.

How often do you run away?
   Where would I go? The earth is sowed in me, I am spread upon the earth. Unfortunately, I recognize myself everywhere.

Have you read the records?
   Just the disasters. Little else interests me.

Why did you choose this speaker?
   She had no shame about decaying. One voice is as good as another for my purposes.

Who are your enemies?
   The noose, the gas, the gun.

Whom have you loved chiefly?
   The liver and kidneys which so quickly replicate, cancer, kudzu that eats, men who hate everything around them.

Whom have you studied under?
   The world. Everyone is my master.

Motorcade

I cannot tell you what dogs chased him, just that he often woke
to their teeth on his skin—One pack he named
Death, one pack he called to him with a whistle.

Unspooled from a wide black place in the earth, they howled
to find him—One pack had haunches made from barbed wire,
one pack gathered heat from the nuclear reactor.

He exiled himself to the edges, out from his own house to wander—
One pack gnawed at the wooden frame of motel doors,
one pack chased the rubber tires of our car.

His fear ran through the desert—cool trail through heat—sky-written
trail in dust. We slept with scissors beneath the bed, we buried
a black-handled knife outside each threshold.

Sometimes he threw the edges of a caught life between them
to scavenge and gnaw at, sometimes he unwound a small piece of film
from inside one of his limbs, fed them part of his immortal memory.

When we stopped, I'd pour gunpowder around his figure on the ground,
his lying form. As we drove away, we'd watch his burning shape in mirrors.
For weeks, maybe good enough—the air silent—but when

they eventually returned, they would tear him apart in their jaws,
backing up from his body to pull meat from a carcass, then
scatter parts of him in the median along the interstate.

There he would lay quiet, nursing growth as if he were the old ship
Theseus made, replaced plank by plank with new wood, until
who could tell what was most his mapped-out body—

the scraps we drove by slowly, marked by iron
crosses and plastic flowers, or the facsimile copy
thrashing and howling in the car while the dogs chased?

The History of Mankind's Errors, the Beautiful and Interesting Extravagancies and Absurdities

Failure pulls a rabbit from a hat, from a lapel. Failure levitates in order:
  Corpse, me, car, motel.

Like produces like, an effect resembles its cause.

Birds go astray. Smudge of red, smudge of yellow, smudge of brown.

The Burned-Over District. Failure loses face.

Failure loses his face, a vast rubbing etched away. An Etch A Sketch, shaken.
  A man in a Proteus box.

Failure eats his words, Failure eats crow, his hat, humble pie, his shoe,
  swallows his foot.

Things which have once been in contact with each other are always in contact.

The gods come at first reluctantly, then more easily when they have formed
  the habit of entering the same person.

Failure's errors set him in motion across the sea. He errants, erratic, he
  roams, astray.

Remake the torn cards, scarves become flowers, birds become the cages
  where they are secreted.

Magicians duplicate the "proofs" of divine intervention.

Law of similarity, law of contagion.

Failure in his developing room quietly splices errors into the flashbulb memories of Kennedy's assassination, the buildings falling.

Craftsperson that he was: that extra carriage, that second shooter in such
lovely shades of rhyming blue.

He changes things subtly: the rabbit, the saw, the dove, the hovering woman.

The rabbit pulls on red kid gloves, begins munching at the sawdust in its
cavities.

Failure through a series of pulleys places the man behind the man's own
back and holds him there for a decade.

With a copy of the little red book and a hat, he places the woman behind her
own back and leads her to the altar.

He hypnotizes the crowd in the floating casino.

We sing in chorus the party line. We tow down the boat in the murky river
and drown.

White Sands: {window, car} {window, motel} {wind, oh} {but, oh} {Butoh}

As we move through the desert—pockmarked:

the winds that blew here, storms of man and light:

glass stars formed from radiation, strewn, gleaming:

he talks of the Butoh, naked actors covered in ash:

their limbs contorted, gnarled, they slowly:

explode or fall, grotesque open mouths, and:

twisted, taut fingers—In their minds they hold:

as a single motivation the flash of brilliance:

bomb made in the city, from the collective:

watching eyes, clothes burned from backs:

and limbs, they hold that year, the shadows:

in the angles of their body, living enactment:

of the made Pompeii, and Failure attends:

every show, moves first:

slowly, through the face of each actor:

then, more deeply down into limbs of the spectators:

settles in those who hear about it, secondhand:

[the god of the living flesh says nothing:

what is harnessed, what is dropped:]

settles in me, until I curl at night into:

a replica of someone, falling, having fallen:

and the lights dangle over Hiroshima, over Kyoto:

Failure's Experiments with Medals

Mistook organs for medals, and so, decorating the bodies for burial, pinned on the lapels of the soldiers the following: kidneys, livers, hearts with ventricles and arteries, above and below, four petals, an arrow, a French or Celtic or Scottish cross, the lungs on either side of the bomber's jacket, looking unfortunately like wax-melted wings, intestine as a military sash—and so the ground festooned with bodies, festooned with the interiors of the bodies on the bodies.

Fugue State

A befuddlement, an aporia, an inky sea:

    Failure worked as an army cryptologist,

        drew maps in the dark of the hold, created languages

            describing: Disasters or weather or weather caused by disasters—

      evolution's slow, dim-witted carnage

    35-mile fish kill in Dunkard Creek, Washington County,

the coarsening of the mind.

Born into deeper drought, fiercer floods, if you gave him a home,

    Failure would hoard animals, coal—carbon-based fuels,

      would turn into laziness, sloth, trickster, that senile old bear who dances for seals.

        Soak them in salt and the trees will die from the top down.

      Willows, wastewater, acetic acid, cotton.

Devastate boreal forests and thaw the tundra.

I would make him a landlocked shipwreck, horses felled by volcanic ash,

would render the human into raw materials: lungs, liver, corneas, & kidneys,

would bury the dogs in graves as their noses and jaws cool.

Completing a project, Failure would stare at his baffled limbs,

all that thrashing trying to contain the motion

his body wanted out of him.

The thawing permafrost releases methane. Deep-change accident, god of the hinge.

Two burns on his chest prove the heart beats but say nothing of the soul.

Failure's Sermon

Having been the tenant farmer of god, having sowed and reaped, boss, when the god went silent I washed his mouth out with dates and honey, when he cursed I washed his mouth with salt water from the ocean, ashes from the dead; I washed his mouth with the blood of this lamb whose throat I cut tenderly out in my field until the red ran out into the seedlings, until the ammonia in the bladder leaked down to the stones—

Inside these barbed-wire rings, I have been the tenant farmer of god, have sowed in the salt of men's bodies his words (from my own throat) let fall, let fall on me (and the trucks run across the freeway and we drive straight into the obscuring smoke), what goes up in flames like formaldehyde, like a man's or woman's intentions together, this plague of words upon your heads—a hundred sign languages echoing each other (in place of the goat's fur, the human, in place of the goat's blood, the audience's tears)

Oh lungs compose the songs
Of my people in concrete

How to Get Along in a Ruined, God-Weakened World

Exuberance followed by melancholy.

To pay for gas, Failure works on the estate: groundskeeper, wrangler,
Land mine, caterer, housekeeper, expert.

The slow inexorable profaning of our species, an indistinct hissing of the idols

If Failure is the tree, you are the gardener too timid to trim, too arthritic to
    climb, too empathetic to chop.

Its roots twine round your legs, become your veins. You are pushed through
    its bark until you are its flower, its fruit, its rotted meat. Now

You are both the one who gathers and the one who eats.
You entice insects with your beauty or acrid odor.

Failure fails to be a house, a child, a stray pet. Failure fails to analogize, to
    anthologize.

I slept with the hallucinated god that I might better be his medium.

You fulfill the Circe in you, you turn into a jackdaw. At night, you hunt
    and eat out your own heart as if it is the hard nut at the heart of a poppy
    flower, bitter and crowned in purple.

Conjugate: the ruin has been ruined by ruin and rain.

His spirit lowers himself into me, I am his horse

Failure plays the bleeding statue: certain engines and old wires, rotten sticks
    in his back

My silhouette in candles, then, once lit and burned, in wax

You would trade every painting of the man for one photograph, proof
Of his long fingers on the wood.

In the flood the gods withdraw from the earth, pull up skirts and boots
And go.

I Can't Succeed at Anything Here So I Can't Prove I Exist

Whiteout = world without shadows.

When it needs to stop the snow will not stop falling on the radio—

Failure remakes himself each morning. No roots, a new thing.

Sometimes still he wakes covered in ice:
a breastplate, a helmet, a gas mask, a pair of boots—

Still-hunting: an attempt to reach silence.

We pass the beautiful distortions of silver, become
Francis Bacons in the steel barrels of the trucks
delivering the sea-borne house coal, the milk.

In cold, the impulse of skin to stick to instruments,
mouths or hands held helplessly open against the metal.

Salt drawings in the snow.
Debacle = tumultuous breakup of ice in a river.

Snow tarnished by the road corrodes like silver—
We push on down the highway.

Museum of snow, permafrost beneath the tundra.

Hunting down the still lifes, enough to make, to still the life.

Failure's Project in Detritus and Disease

If for the warrior, soul is coughed from the mouth,   if from horses disease proceeds from the mouth,
while birds migrating shit on everything,   cover the world in germ,   then the soul can be bled out through
a wound, also the microbe, also the will.   If from the lungs   comes the blood which drowns

evacuated villages, burning tires   If from the lungs comes the prophecy of Delphi   from her
frenzied body,   various contortions of the mouth   And Frankfurt doctors said *blood pours*
from all the apertures   And the hospital surrounded by the white gauze of bandage as warning.

If the cough in horses spreads influenza;   if it escaped from a body and leapt here,   mosquitoes carry
yellow plague; water holds   cholera; diptheria: airborne; tuberculosis: airborne; Spanish flu closes
down theaters; smallpox through saliva   If the city covers homes   and streets in lime dust

Of the far-flinging body of the disease, sing praise through the boundless earth, the molten body   Those
who heal with distinct poxing, those who grow new skin   Forge the tissue of the disease to make an
antibody   Forge the tissue of the paper to form a god   If from the huts of the infected

who'd vomited black blood,   Failure carries out a corpse he'd prepare for burial,   spreads plague

at funerals licking shut condolence   cards, disease leaking from the casket we held   If we burn huts

that held ailing bodies   If we burn ailing bodies that held loud minds   And ash rises from the city and

the altar, bow down   Among scattered contaminated syringes that shine, bow down   And the birds

write us messages on the sky, leaving behind them germ,   And the gods write to us inside the birds—

windpipe, lungs, liver, gall bladder, coils of intestines—   We wait for priests to whisper in the ear

of the animal before the sacrifice,   Before they open the bodies of the birds   To deliver their urgent messages.

Failure's Artificial Heart

To give him what he would need to keep the dogs at bay,
the Corpse & I scavenged every metal from the machines
with a hammer—icemakers in motels, abandoned cars, computers
in the dump, densified cans,

                              wire, oil drums, filters,
ferrous scraps from useful things—until we'd gleaned
enough copper to coat the whole body
to make an antenna of the flesh—

                    We laid down
orange rinds and pomegranates, made of Failure's body
an altar for doctors to lay the sacrifice on.

To receive the heart, first exchange:
Iceberg for the transmitter,

                              the continuous flow pump;
Mittens for the soft furry shine of the heart's skin;
In the pits we dug we buried mortars and pestles,

                              sickle blades to appease the earth;
The soft neck of the goat for the valve,

                              risen god-house for the soft tubing.

Packed in the iceberg, he lay part flayed
open by the scalpel. Divine hallucinations in the anesthesia
of gods in scrubs attending the blade, overheard
voice of the dead king.

                              While his heart lay in the surgeon's hands,
he was half man, half deer, he was peeled back and turned inside out—
For days he chirped and beeped

                              where other men ticked he whirred.

I went to fetch him from the honeycombed Arctic. From the ship's deck
I watched ice crumble, flow like lava into water.

On the black sand of the seashore, icebergs cast up small effigies
of their kind.

                        We spoke in sign language for days,
his hand against his body to mean something—
and when he was thirsty, I would chip away
                        part of the ice he was packed in
and bring it to his lips. In this way,
                        he gradually licked his way out of the cold.

The furry humming creature inside of him moved his blood
with a small magnet.
                        When I put my ear against his chest, I could hear
nothing, then the sea. He put his ear against my chest to entertain himself
with time. That clumsy thumping thing, beast he warmed
                        his icy hands against.

Failure and I Bury the Body

Down a mine shaft throw the Corpse
Spread his ashes over the ashes of the trailer
Go to the fire-ravaged lot and inter him in the record
of the blaze, formaldehyde walls, coffee tin intact

Like roadkill parcel him out for birds
Along the highways along its shoulders
we muscle down, out his limbs from the trunk, from the truck bed

We banner nails across the surface of his body and leave him in the lightning
    field
We bury him face down to be shamed by the living

To hold him under bathtub water, I straddle him
with my hand against his chest
the way I held my hand against him once
to leverage my own body's rocking

We sell him to the army for land-mine experiments
Cast a hundred mud copies and leave them to decay in a field

With the microscopic saw we water-thin wafer him and pass him out on the
    streets
Wrapped in black plastic and secured with gray duct tape, we let him tour
cadaver shows, let doctors practice rare procedures in his flesh
We leave him at the body farm to join the recording project

He refuses to hold, catch, stay dead, buried, decompose
Always at the cave rolling back the rock, at the door
in the morning, holding out the newspaper, in the afternoons
ripping strips from it to sculpt the latest conflict
in papier-mâché and spit.

Failure and I Bury the Body, Redux

OK, so once we coated him in sulfur
and dragged him behind us across the road like a match—
had I hated him, had he been living,
this would have been unspeakable
but all we wanted was to make him
a spectacle to remember himself by,

Ditto the race car on the track, switch smoke, burned tires and sculpted
    metal

We put him in the catfish pond as feed

We placed his body too close to the river to run to silt

When it froze: outside in the field
When it thawed: deep in the earth

His eyes stayed closed, calm
while his body, intact, survived
one element after another

We paid to have him thrown from a plane, into a lake, to catch in a tree
We made him a pendulum hanging from the bridge's beams

Lit the projector's carbon, burned him down in a celluloid fire
so that he played across the movie screen, left him
in the prison yard, beside a drug deal, down the chimney
of a nuclear reactor, downstream
from Three Mile Island, in the Pittsburgh coal fire pits,
in the river Cuyahoga

We tried to disappear him, to forget him, to keep by forgetting—
That self-observed-self continues/runs/parses/echoes out a living in my body

We dragged him into the ravine, propped his rifle on the rock,
turned his quiet face to the camera

We built him a monument and held the door for him to enter, we made him
a small puppet theater in the vast wilderness and drove away.

True North

Failure: allegory of the shipwreck, cast up on desert

Shipwreck of atomic light in the desert, Crusoe in the fake villages

(at the end of the bones of the ship: desiccated bodies in the sand

made maw and mark in earth—in salt—)

Inferior mirage: slick on the dry road

Superior mirage: objects lifted above the obscuring curvature of the Earth

A small boat, catastrophe across one sea to another,

You drown in the black tar, you feel suffocated by the press

of desert stars, all around you temperatures are rising

like a tide that won't recede, you pool the boat, you push away the water

Like a magician, the sea levitates the image of an iceberg, ships,
        a continent—

We sail into another false fire.

Arctic mirage: when the Corpse held me, the sea lifted

my other self from the icy underworld

And held it above me

In the field of vision

Where belief occurs.

Deep here at night, the cold descends

enough to feel like a god,

One perturbed and bovine eye staring down.

Thou Art Thou

I planned our wedding while Failure soldered out the beast and stitched its uniform for waltzing. Failure would like to play the priest. Failure would like to play

the accordion. To go before a judge to say "I do" is to be made legal certainly in the sight of wood paneling and perhaps a wooden pew. The metronomes on shelves around the room

tick out the words, couple by couple. The Corpse promised to stand up for him. Failure stitched himself together attendant groomsmen from the animals.

In my bridal finery, motel curtain as veil, borrowed coat to cover the dress, I arrived in a boat held by the Corpse on stilts, a camel's back made winged.

New old buried blue.

Failure read the fairy tale as the breaking of glass under the shoe and broke the glass shoe, under his heel with the pop of champagne—under the canopy a single pea, a single

feather—take inside you this hope, this levitating balloon. First we threw the salamander into the family hearth, from the light cast back we conflated each part of our two shadows.

At the feast, we tricked bees into thinking we were strange flowers so they will remember our faces. I kissed the Protean in him. His stories bed down in me.

After the ceremony, to seal the deal, Failure wrapped a snow globe depicting Antarctica in his handkerchief and smashed it with his foot.

Under the ice, our two selves wed and wed and wed.

Failure's Coat of Birds

Failure hums]with the[swarm of birds around him, them, loft
of carcasses pulsing]not seen wings like insects but made jewel[taken
like gems around the throat, a coat, a beekeeper wrapped
]in the chain mail of stinger and stripe, replicated & replicated[around him
hums the living thing, he fades into movement blur of wings
then]comes clear[as through a sliver of curtain parted, furious
hunger that plunges a long beak of sight]am beak, weak about the knees[
into the flowers]indiscriminate and red[how is this supposed
to teach me about the world? He says compared to this, you are
a vast stillness, you move glacially and stall, you cannot have
you cannot]and around him the hum rises, overflows
the room with its tinny heater, the hum floods
the smallness of me and vibrates[take nothing
and spend it on the winged gems]glass & battery[to tempt
him with, then replace slowly, till he accumulates around him
the whirr of tiny machines] [that one day fail, simultaneously,
and fall like blossoms to the burnt umber carpet of the motel floor.

Transformation

In the wilderness prepare thee

Because I am broken I can be permeable

In the wilderness

Because I am empty I can be filled

Prepare the wilderness

In the wild mind

The brambles catch fleeting thoughts

In the storms that will undo, prepare thee

And when I have nothing,
              I will give you my hair

Corpse's Lullaby

How long would it take to wrap my lover's body in red string

       How many skeins and how numb the bending fingers when done

           How long would it take to weave my hair between the hairs of his body

I could not give him a liver or a kidney, a lung or a tooth

       Like a lump of payment between us, I gave him nothing

           To record, nothing of note. I gave him nothing in the shape

of an aorta, sliced from my chest with a sure and delicate motion

       I gave him the nothing that fell like blown cotton from the sky and disappeared

It took years to dismantle our house together, with each plank to sliver the planes

       down into fine and bendable vines, years to turn the house from something solid

           into something woven and curved, a set of abstract and fleshy haunches

in wood. There, across the prairie, rising from the peat, it stands. My love is my love

       and he moves through the spaces I left open in the weaving. He returns

           to the nothing I made him and lays down there on the idea of my body.

Superior Mirage

Shackleton wonders: what is that glow on the horizon?
It is the body of Dido burning: There sets the bulk of my love.

One day, the Corpse had no life in him. Odd
to say of a dead thing, been dead
for many months, but he was done with it and we knew.

For days we tried to revive his interest
in the masquerade of roadside shops, in reappearing
in the night. But he was now
just object, his mute thoughts gone elsewhere.

That motel was the loneliest place to die, Failure like a dog curled
at the foot of the floral bedspread, curled like a dog on the floor for vigil.

When the blossom broke through, we found the bud was false—then fruit
replaced the wrongness of the blossom

We realized death had been long stuck
In his throat, a certain hoarseness he was
finally able to clear with his regurgitations, his incessant cough

To speak of failure, since I can only speak of lack.

Why doesn't the body wear away with tears? Why not like sandstone? Like
    bones in a lake? With lapping?

In the snow they came upon a small pile of clothes,
But for the blood, like the vision of spontaneous combustion

Through the animals' flesh, the man was transmuted as flesh—

God bless you, God bathe you in blood.

Let go.

Make a fire pit in the form of a body, a human mound in grass.

Freezing Water. Wind.

In my mind I lived there once happily, content to wake under the
    claustrophobic press of the cloudless sky—the agoraphobic sweep
    of the sea—

The boys go down to the lake, the boys go down to the sea.

Schoolroom covered in the light dusting of asbestos & plaster, room
with edges chewed at.

(If beauty rises from the earth, what is there to do but kill it, kill it?)

Something that could hold us in its savage belly till we die—
I made nothing of nothing.

Here I am with a bridle in my hand and my tongue clicking—

I was the single gesture he made from ear to cunt with his hand and
    how he dragged
me down into him.

Fill the buckets with salt to toss into the storm clouds—
Faces up, we drink a sea from the raindrops.

Hoping I am right I have been carved away from him like a rib,
Like pulling a ship from one bottle and reassembling it in another.

Like a ship's prow—without me,
who will fit inside the glass of his body?

A Brave, Generous Passion

As a child, I called the birds down from the sky, they fell on and around us, and my mother said what lovely stones and she held them in her mouth and sucked then spit them into the dirt and buried them.

Below the earth, the birds grew and erupted with the force of tulips; for years they called into themselves the means to fly from the insects in the fields, swallowed liquid and stones to hold in their gullets—deep water structure, deep aerial structure—the smaller birds on the larger to hide, the smaller in the feathers to hide—one bird perched in the mouth of another to eat from its throat.

When the Corpse died, the trees were bare, I killed with an ax the bird we had been feeding, I held the beheaded bird against my body to mark me with its dying. I covered myself in feathers to make the soul a small humanoid bird, to become something transcendent. The trees were bare, I called down the birds from the sky, my heart was bare and like that, bloodied with what I'd done, I sang to them in a long glowing note of mourning.

I Only Am Escaped Alone to Tell Thee

The audience for the service is a man who cannot hear it

The images of the man shown back to his body

In gold covered with roses, with myrrh, with what we know
to give of the world, left,
we leave him the bounty

If you watched him with desire, you watched him with pity

I only am escaped
alone to tell thee

If you sing for him, the song will lap at his body inside the box, will
    move him

The fire has fallen on the sheep and made of them sacrifice

(though he cannot be called back, the beautiful lie says he is with you)

We give him everything he needed
to hear, We wait, we give it to him

Being beside his body, the chill increases

Feeling of headlights passing over you
as you stand behind a window in the dark.

Now, after the last day, we give him

what he waited to, what he cannot hear

Burial

Hot mind of radiation—

Failure illuminates the Corpse in layers—gilded muscles, nerves with the
flourish of leaves

Failure reanimates the Corpse with electricity.

How delicious in high summer for the body to shudder in a breeze

Like an accordion, the waxing and waning of life.

Failure billows air into the dead lungs.

The sentence gives you the motion but not the thought.

As a final tribute, we record all his inner workings, we weigh the organs on
the scale,

Heart lungs liver bowels kidney

Jar them in formalin and Tupperware

Before we lay him finally,

Gently down

Into the ground.

Memorials:

{Death appears and stuffs the body with mothballs}

{Plant snow globes across the yard in winter—snow presses on the glass
until they break}

{Military uniforms folded like the ceremonial flag, triangles cased in black}

{Pack what you wish to save in the salt of the sea}

{Each organ in a drawer of the card catalogue}

{A card catalogue filled with the typing of his name}

{Write his biography in sugared ink and leave the manuscript in a field for
ants, who will eat away the letters so light breaks through}

{With twine, string one hundred golden hens across the telephone wire
above the street to twirl in the wind, blinking}

{Douse the wall of lightbulbs in gasoline and strike the match
to release their shining}

[On Set: Weight of Flame, Transcendence of Smoke.]

The sun's evidence appears before its body emerges—and lingers after.

Failure recalls mornings on a burning bus. Was it a riot or a looting? Was it a coup or a machine's misstep? He won't say. He makes himself crow and jackal.

Lord of the birds.

Dust loose in the sky like a storm of locusts.

[No record of two cars on fire, of a woman trapped, but a pile of plastic flowers and an iron cross.]

[No record of the truck fire but a halo of grass made acidic, engine salting earth.]

The stop signs strung on the string of vision, passing, red beads of the rosary.

We've lasted this long, outpacing the slow radiation of our flaws.

Redux

Do you take this person whole through blunder and triumph, do you take this person broken in darkened rooms and abandoned fields, do you take this person luminous with the burn of love and grief?

Yes, again, yes, what else is there?

The female Elvis impersonator readjusts the wig over her blond hair.

Wax flowers, darling, velvet drapes.

Circle around me seven times and lift the veil.

Elvis in velvet blesses us.

They ladle kerosene into the lamp out of habit or tenderness.

The greenhouses with windows of mica cast watery light
onto the orange trees, hung with brilliant weight.

Failure kisses me as chastely as a brother.

Golden Mean

The dead cat, the rabbit carcass aloft.
      Hanging over the fence, the jagged leaves
            between the lamps of golden fruit—
a wedding, a wake, a wakefulness.
      Along the roads of Vietnam/Iraq, sound sensors
          planted in the war register
nothing they were supposed to—perhaps
      a migration of birds, perhaps
           a storm coming from the mountains;
meanwhile the armies march and recede
      the men make percussion on the ground
         with their bodies.
We dust the oranges with pesticide
      that bees feather over the flowers,
         they drop like swollen fruit
honey stuck in their bellies—A ducked chin
      a V of hair in the back, we watch
         the photos for signs of life:
the act of unconcealing—a watchfulness and ticking.
      I trade three oranges for the bayonet
         melt the sword down to a ring,
use the wood for a stake our tree will climb.
      The fruit hangs over the fence
         from the neighbors' yard where they
poison bees and play the most beautiful music.
      We bury the dead cat, we cover
         our faces in the blood of the rabbit.
To understand what love has made of us
      golden, jagged, and swollen—
         we drape our bodies across the fences;
We climb more deeply into the light of the sun.

Remade

The sheep rings the bell quietly while it eats
with the motion of its jaw, the clapper swings

Gravity pulls the rivers down to the oceans

Snow falls on the bare shorn sheep

No vacancies tonight, we sleep in the car
To entertain me, he calls up northern lights on his skin
(waves of violent light, driven across the sky)

The icebergs shear off, tumble
like sinking ships

Leaning against his chest, I almost hear the noise and cracking of the
    thunder of a fire.

Like another mountain range lit in the desert
in this heating world

When I saw the bison fall, what an ache, but underneath their skins at night
    with him, what pleasure

We have made peace with it, with the world

Failure who at night is a corpse made of bees

We will look for new earth to plant, a sod roof sprouting

—the linear sentence proceeds and falls—what you came to, you see on
    your own—

Pasture: strewn, small packs—sat & held to ground like low squat beasts and
   grazed voracious for everything tender

All the clover hanging from the mouths

We will begin human history, again.

Failure's Accounting of Influences

"Forge with the Stars of Distant Fire":
Gary H. Holthaus, *Wide Skies*

"Yes, That Year":
Harper's "Findings," October 2009 and May 2010; Aristophanes, *The Birds;*
Rebecca Solnit, *River of Shadows: Eadweard Muybridge and the Technological Wild West*

"True North":
Cy Twombly book; Glenn Gould; Josh Fox's film *Gasland;* Roald Amundsen;
Ginger Strand, "Why Look at Fish?," *The Believer,* February 2005

"Using a Fleshing Machine":
Title from Susan Orlean, "Lifelike," *The New Yorker,* June 9, 2003

"Tanks of Fluid Converted to Motion":
Hilton Als, "True Stories," *The New Yorker,* August 20 and 27, 2001

"We Visit Every Nursing Home from Amarillo to Yuma":
Rainer Maria Rilke, "Primal Sound"

"As It Appears Underneath a Cloud, Failure & I Drive
Towards the Underbelly of the Sun":
Jeffrey Eugenides, *Middlesex*

"Failure Moves Through the Wolf's Hide; as Death, Covers the Boat":
Anthony Lane, "Breaking the Waves," *The New Yorker,* April 12, 1999; Kathyrn
Schulz, *Being Wrong*

"In re: Failure, Body Where Tar and Light Meet":
Book of Joshua; Jon Mooallem, "A Curious Attraction," *Harper's,*
October 2007;

"Machine That Leaves and Never Returns":
David Samuels, "Wild Things," *Harper's,* June 2012; Yves Klein

"Failure Dreams of Elements":
Mary Jacobus, "Is There a Woman in This Text?" from *Reading Woman: Essays in Feminist Criticism*

"Project for a Machine for Grasping":
Steve Featherstone, "Life in the Zone," *Harper's,* June 2011; Kathyrn Schulz, *Being Wrong;* title from Yves Klein

"Partage: Dividing of the Spoils":
Mark Levine

"The Agonizing Blue of the Sky":
Félix Guattari; Kathyrn Schulz, *Being Wrong*

"Failure tends to fall":
Werner Herzog, *Encounters at the End of the World*

"I Tell Failure the True Story of the Corpse":
Josh Fox, *Gasland*

"In Return, Failure Tells Me Stories":
Kathyrn Schulz, *Being Wrong;* Rebecca Solnit, *River of Shadows: Eadweard Muybridge and the Technological Wild West;* Bill Buford, *Walton Ford: Panch Tantra*

"Annotated Plans for an Evacuation":
Harper's "Findings," November 2009; title from Alex Hubbard

"Project for a Machine for the End of Civilization":
Title from Yves Klein

"Failure on the Theme of the Ruined Landscape":
Edward Burtynsky; Rebecca Solnit, *River of Shadows: Eadweard Muybridge and the Technological Wild West*

"An Emaciated Horse Led by His Master":
Title from Alice Neel; Whittaker Chambers; Saint Augustine, *Confessions*

"Agriculture Begins":
Lewis Hyde, *The Gift;* Laurie Garrett, *The Coming Plague;* Francis Bacon

"Failure Burns the Taxidermy Museum":
Susan Orlean, "Lifelike," *The New Yorker,* June 9, 2003

"Fecundity, Expanse":
Svetlana Boym, "Paradise Misplaced," *Harper's,* March 2001; Ana Mendiata

"The Learned World, the Conversable World":
David Hume; Kevin Kelly in an interview: "Tending the Garden of Technology" *Orion* (Jan/Feb 2010)

"The Failure of Sequestration":
Laurie Garrett, "Cherynobyl's Lessons for Japan," *New York Times* op-ed, March 17, 2011; Steve Featherstone, "Life in the Zone," *Harper's,* June 2011; IAEA training book

"Baptize the Long-Dead":
Ulysses S. Grant; Julian Jaynes, *The Origin of Consciousness in the Breakdown of the Bicameral Mind;* Laurie Garrett, *The Coming Plague*

"Failure's Beatitudes":
Francine Prose, "You Got Eyes: Robert Frank Imagines America," *Harper's,* January 2010, William T. Vollman, "Letter from Kirkuk," *Harper's,* April 2010

"On Set: The West":
Gary H. Holthaus, *Wide Skies*

"We Prepare for the Coming Blackouts":
Ginger Strand, "Why Look at Fish?," *The Believer,* February 2005; Henry Darger; Pindar; "Trial by Fire," *Texas Monthly,* December 2011

"INTERVIEW (VERSO)":

Harper's "Findings," June 2009; William H. Gass "Kinds of Killing," *Harper's*, August 2009

"MOTORCADE":

Ana Mendiata

"THE HISTORY OF MANKIND'S ERRORS, THE BEAUTIFUL AND INTERESTING EXTRAVAGANCIES AND ABSURDITIES":

Benjamin Franklin; James Frazer *The Golden Bough*; Julian Jaynes *The Origin of Consciousness in the Breakdown of the Bicameral Mind*

"FUGUE STATE":

Lewis Hyde, *Trickster Makes This World: Mischief, Myth, and Art*; Cy Twombly

"FAILURE'S SERMON":

Pindar; Julian Jaynes, *The Origin of Consciousness in the Breakdown of the Bicameral Mind*; Lewis Hyde, *The Gift*

"HOW TO GET ALONG IN A RUINED, GOD-WEAKENED WORLD":

Julian Jaynes, *The Origin of Consciousness in the Breakdown of the Bicameral Mind*

"I CAN'T SUCCEED AT ANYTHING HERE SO I CAN'T PROVE I EXIST":

Gary H. Holthaus *Wide Skies*; Rebecca Solnit, *River of Shadows: Eadweard Muybridge and the Technological Wild West*

"FAILURE'S PROJECT IN DETRITUS AND DISEASE":

Julian Jaynes, *The Origin of Consciousness in the Breakdown of the Bicameral Mind*; Laurie Garrett, *The Coming Plague*

"FAILURE'S ARTIFICIAL HEART":

Julian Jaynes *The Origin of Consciousness in the Breakdown of the Bicameral Mind*

"Failure and I Bury the Body":
Annie Cheney "Resurrection Men: Scenes from the Cadaver Trade,"
Harper's March 2004

"True North":
Kathyrn Schulz, *Being Wrong;* James Joyce, *Portrait of the Artist as a Young Man*

"Thou Art Thou":
Harper's, "Findings," April 2010

"Superior Mirage":
Hegel; Sophie Calle

"A Brave, Generous Passion":
Ana Mendiata; Julian Jaynes, *The Origin of Consciousness in the Breakdown of the Bicameral Mind*

"Memorials":
Robert ParkeHarrison

"Golden Mean":
Joseph Beuys

Acknowledgments

Many thanks to the editors at the following journals where these poems first appeared: *32 Poems, B O D Y, Green Mountains Review, The Journal, New Madrid, Redivider, r.kv.r.v.y., Salt Hill, Sonora Review, The Southern Review, Third Coast,* and *West Branch.*

For giving me physical space to work: Taffy and Martin Kim, Jeff Fort and the late Marion Barthelme, and Marsha Recknagel. Without a residency at Madroño Ranch, this manuscript could not have found its final form. I'll be forever grateful to Heather and Martin Kohout for that gift.

For support of this and previous projects: Houston Arts Alliance, Rice University's Parks Fellowship, Michael and Nina Zilkha, the Verlaine Prize, UH, everyone at Inprint and at *Gulf Coast: A Journal of Literature and Fine Arts,* and the wonderful folks at Bread Loaf Writers' Conference: especially Michael Collier, Noreen Cargill, Jennifer Grotz, Amaud Jamaul Johnson, Paul Yoon, Jason Schneiderman, Robin Ekiss, K. Bradford, and team Voltron.

For shepherding this book into being: D. Nurkse, the National Poetry Series and Stephanie Stio, and everyone at HarperCollins, especially Michael Signorelli.

For being kind and useful voices in my head: Brigit Pegeen Kelly, Tom Sleigh, Nick Flynn, Claudia Rankine, Matthea Harvey, Carl Phillips, Matt Hart, Mark Doty, and Allen Grossman.

For support, feedback, and friendship throughout: Emily Perez, Jill Meyers, Nina McConigley, Leslie Harrison, Hallie Smith, Monica Parle, Melissa McCrimmon, and Junko Io. All of you amaze me. Thanks also to my colleagues at Rice University, especially Susan Wood and Joe Campana, and at the LBJ School of Public Affairs. Gratitude for all the amazing students I've had over the years who have inspired me with their words and their labor.

For my mother, who copied down my first poem and never stopped listening. For my father and my family, which has grown to include people I love so dearly, including Martin, Kathe MacLaren, and all the Clarks.

Most of all, for Charlie, whose luminous mind and heart make venturing into the wilderness possible. Your deep kindness gives me bravery.